AF604793

the Flower Garden

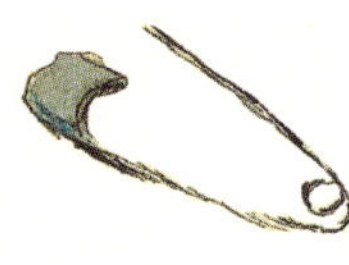

To those who support and guide us ~CS

To Zia Angela, who makes magic with needles and hooks ~LM

The Flower Garden: A Changi Secret
First published in 2026
by Walker Books Australia Pty Ltd
Gadigal and Wangal Country
Locked Bag 22, Newtown
NSW 2042 Australia
www.walkerbooks.com.au

Walker Books Australia acknowledges the Traditional Owners of the country on which we work, the Gadigal and Wangal peoples of the Eora Nation, and recognises their continuing connection to the land, waters and culture. We pay our respect to their Elders past and present.

A catalogue record for this book is available from the National Library of Australia

ISBN: 978 1 760657 35 2

The illustrations for this book were created using watercolour and ink
Typeset in Carre Noir Pro
Printed and bound in China

EU Authorized Representative: HackettFlynn Ltd,
36 Cloch Choirneal, Balrothery, Co. Dublin, K32 C942, Ireland.
EU@walkerpublishinggroup.com

10 9 8 7 6 5 4 3 2 1

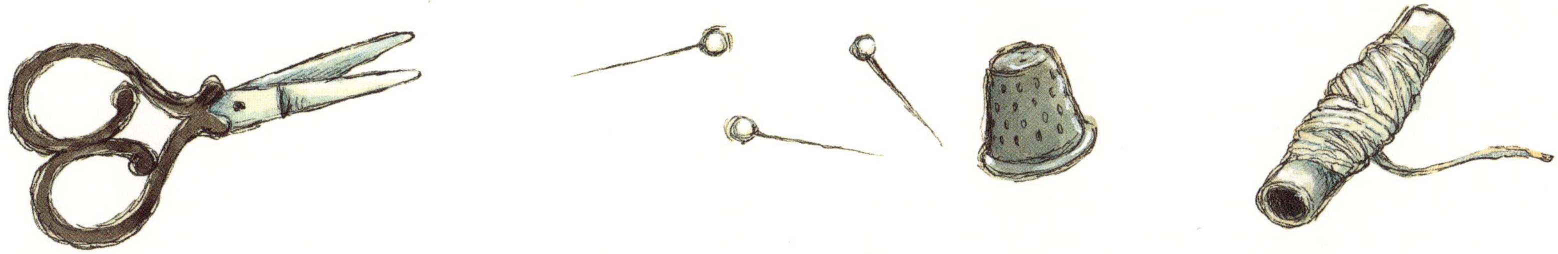

the Flower Garden

A CHANGI SECRET

CLAIRE SAXBY and LUCIA MASCIULLO

WALKER BOOKS
AND SUBSIDIARIES
LONDON • BOSTON • SYDNEY • AUCKLAND

I have a secret –

we have a secret –

in this place where secrets
are not allowed.

It's for Mrs Ennis

who showed us how to soar,

how to leave the locked-up chattering,

lose ourselves in patterned stars.

She showed us how to sew,

a stitch for
every task.

She said cut the day in pieces,

trim long hours
with your threads.

My friends and I and Julia
beg and borrow what we can.

We scavenge blues and yellows,

faded reds

and tattered greens.

Mornings, we work in heat-hazed lines,

dig and turn and weed and stake,

strain our backs, stain our fingers,

grow food we'll never eat.

We sit in rows all afternoon –

recite numbers,
words and formulas,

sing songs of freedom fading.

Softly, softly now.

After dinner, dishes clear away
and dusk pulls in the breeze,

mothers settle babies
and at last, the time is ours.

We hide in cornered shadows,

stitch side by side by side.

Flowers grow from our fingers

and we write our names in twisted thread.

We listen for our captors,
their random swoop and seize.

I jump at every footstep.
We flutter with each skit or shuffle.

A sudden black-boot clatter
is enough to race our hearts

as guards clomp round the corner
too late to see a thing.

We skim sheets, slips, skirts and shirts.

Snip, snap!

The scraps take shape,

set flowers in a wandering path

of mixed and stitched pale patches.

It's time to gather party food.

We do the best we can,

whisper party invitations,

hold tight to our surprise.

For all that you have shown us,
for all the skills we've learned,
for all you did to save us,

Happy Birthday, Mrs Ennis!

Author's note

After the fall of Singapore in February 1942 of World War II, Japanese invaders imprisoned more than three hundred women and children in Changi Prison. Men were imprisoned nearby in a separate prison. Women and children worked each day in gardens tending vegetables that would only be eaten by their captors. Their prison housed six times the number of inmates it was designed for. Teachers set up classes for the children and taught what they could, although history and geography were banned and their captors watched them closely. One woman, Mrs Ennis, set up a Girl Guide group, to help pass the long, difficult days of their imprisonment. The Changi Girl Guide quilt – which looks like a flower garden – was made by the children as a gift for Elizabeth Ennis for her birthday.

The Changi Girl Guide quilt inspired the creation of the more well-known Red Cross quilts, which were made of individual patches and donated to the Changi hospital.

The quilt that inspired this story is a real quilt. It was donated by the family of Elizabeth Ennis to the Imperial War Museums and can be seen at: www.iwm.org.uk/collections/item/object/30088773